Throwing
~ the ~
Bones

Throwing
~ the ~
Bones

CAITLIN JACKSON

atmosphere press

Table of Contents

*"Among twenty snowy mountains,
The only moving thing
Was the eye of the blackbird."*

-Wallace Stevens

Epigenetic

Trauma can travel
through 13 generations
entrenched in us
on a cellular level.

We carry our ancestor's fear,
jump at loud noises,
struggle to breathe in crowds.

And somewhere in my bones
on a rocky highland
a forefather sits
watching a brook
navigate its stones
and throwing back whiskey
until the moon is high
and the world makes sense
and the memories of blood
splattered slate
are thrown in the water
flowing through time
to the present
where I see red
when I close my eyes.

Talking Board

When I had the magic of 14
in my fingertips
I squandered it all
on questions about boys' feelings.
I watched wide-eyed the trembling tip
of the planchette
as it lied to me.

If it had moved on its own
it would have told me NO would always be my answer.

We drank a gallon of grape juice
and stumbled in the street
pretending to be drunk.
Soon I would not have to pretend
nearly ever again
for 16 whole years.

And ghosts don't have any answers to spell out,
neither can stars hold our wishes
and when I write my fears down on slips of paper
and burn each one
I am not any braver after.

Still nothing can explain my nightmares
the whispers I hear in a shuffled deck of cards
or the centuries-old words that come to me
suddenly
when I pause to recite a spell
just a small one
to the snowy sky.

Good Bones

And I never thought I would be here
prone on a metal table at 36
a doctor deep in me
nose wrinkled all focus on
snagging flesh with his little
plastic harpoon.
There will be no waiting for no counting of
ten tiny perfect toes for me.

You walk away angry
and there is that familiar hole
worn in your back pocket.
It isn't fair to say you've done this to me
but here we are.

And it is almost noon
out west shadows
are disappearing into soles of boots.
Bells are tolling.
The air is breathless, impatient
the trigger is twitching.

Many compass points east
and centuries past
an old man in China smells gunpowder too
as he packs his rocket full of bright red fortune
and sparkling dragon teeth.
There is a hole in his back pocket.

And outside a young woman,
who never thought she would be here,
in this deep,
leaves her baby girl, all shiny penny new,
at the wishing well.
She wiggles her ten perfect toes in the moonlight.

You keep walking, out the door.
The gun fires and slaps the waiting air.
The man's rocket explodes,
the dragon bursts forth in scarlet sparks.
The baby wails a final cry.

And the woman, her way lit by a dim lamp,
and the sky full of celebration,
stumbles in the river
on her way home.
As she falls, she reaches
for my dangling hand,
fingers touching across centuries—
good bone to good bone—

We both pull hard and then
we are sitting up
the metal table frigid beneath our thighs
the world spinning violent around
our grip tight on each other's knuckles.

We look up squinting in exam room lights
and with one voice we say

"Oh yes. We are fine. "

Heart

Even if you do not think you have
you have read of the white hart.
He, ghost-bound, wanders through
your deepest woods
his thin antlers thickening the brush
his hoofbeats rapping messages
into the mossy earth.

You have heard this story
though maybe not seen
quite this picture. You still know it.
Especially the ending
when the white among the green
is snuffed out, and red blots the ground.

You know the ending
because the hunter in the story
is always you.
But then
so is the deer.

Magic

I break away for an afternoon spell
of time on the melting ice.
I'm itching but the bars and Dairy Queen
are closed for the season.

Summer will come but first cruel Spring.

Waves call to us, wind
on our cheeks.
We'll take a boat to the ocean one day
and find wine-dark waters that glow.

You are my ocean love
I will swim in you to shore.

Another Blood Poem

The girl sliced up her legs
with a shaving razor.
I did not take that chance,
wore leggings every day.
And at first they watched me
on camera all night long,
just in case I started to seize—
grasping with both hands
at the empty air.

I stared a long time
at her bloody bandages,
she rolled them up and down again,
as their talk swirled around me
like I was a drain.

Down down down
flowing at last to the ocean.

Promise

This morning a boy danced
at the front of the room
coherent joy rolled off his hips.
I laughed but was afraid.

Please let him get to be older!

And the room sang with him
for a minute all
in the same breath of buoyant air,
fingers stretching towards—

After taking my pills in one hard shot
I went to my room and cried a little.

Outside the sun was pointed.
The heat was rising.
I splashed water on my face
and went back out.

Last Night I Dreamt I Went to Manderley Again

I cried for you all night long
and woke up alone.
I am entering a deep dark fog.

People say addiction is like this
five steps in
ten back out.
Addicts like their sayings gift-wrapped,
throw your keys beneath your bed at night
wake up on your knees.

But I am a wild forest.
Concern is wet and heavy,
someone is panting on my neck.
I tried to leave breadcrumbs
to find my way back
my monsters ate them, red-eyed and gnashing.

Pick a future
they told us in school
who do you want to be?

Circle the pilot
fireman
doctor
teacher—
mother
my aunts, my grandmother, my mom
all made their selections neat and certain.

But where is my picture?
An old woman with long velvet sleeves
pacing up and down stone hallways
her candle
setting fire to grand tapestries
hanging along her path.

She is not there.
I circled mother on the sheet
now I see our kids only in dreams
they leap overboard
I open my mouth but
too late—they're gone

like you in the morning
my fingers brushing empty sheets.

The Singing Bone

A brother killed a brother
and buried him underneath a bridge.

How is that possible?
But now I know,
under enough strain,
even brothers warp and twist.

Goats and people crossed the river
skipping to and fro for many years
until the brother,
the dead one, began to sing.

Or maybe it was a head
floating along a stream
watching fauns wail and
lions weep.

Or maybe it was me
alone in the house, microphone
pressed to lips,
ruptured pop songs spilling
all over my voice.
They are always about love.

It was the bone
they discovered, the men
and the goats. They dug it up
and it lay in the palm of their hand
singing about love
in my broken voice.

Children, what do we think
is the moral of the story?

Safe only to say there was death
and then there was song
and not the other way around.

7IIs

The sun is cooking us all.
We talk wistfully of Diet Coke
or cheeseburgers
but who are we fooling?
(Besides ourselves, kind of.)
We're thinking of wine
or vodka or gin
or powder or needles—
the color orange.

Boat rides are traps
birthdays become dangerous.
I watch the boy
in the American flag shorts
dive into the sand
of the volleyball court
while an unshaven man
strums and sings about loneliness.
We are all well acquainted,
which is strange
since we always had company.
We're here to shake it
to be alone in our minds again.

But it's scary out in the bright sun—
suddenly clear-headed and eyes
focusing, while our brains
whisper seductively
Just a little bit
won't hurt.

Liquid

Feeling cooped up, walls
that used to cradle when I was
exploring other worlds
through gin now I feel them
move to spit me out,
disgusted by my new flavor.

I like the way birds hop
when they're curious.

I will play on moonlight like it is violin strings
except I cannot play the violin
and it is not nighttime.

I want to go out into dark waters
already having had several
sweet concoctions, and do flips
in the ocean until
the sky and the seafloor
are in the same place.

Call Me Al

I hid my bottles on my bookshelf
behind Paul Simon's glossy face.
Once I paused to read his words
but nothing in them stuck.
I was blurry, fading in and out.

I liked having the courage
to stumble through the house
the world waltzing with me.
I would wake up with bruises on my hip—

once my friends dropped me on a tree root.
I remember, the ground was very cold in February.

In the morning my wound was deep
and bright with blood.
I pulled up my shirt
and stared in the mirror for hours
feeling pain when I pressed at my bone.

You ask me to count my bottles
want to know when and where
most of all why. I cannot answer
except I wanted to dance
with the world again.

And that I've learned they'll always drop you
and the dirt will be freezing when you hit it.

Whiskey Ranch

I'm calling to you down a crowded
dream hallway, all the walls are brown
and naturally there is no answer
your head does not even tilt
a little toward my voice.

And last night I cried
after, in bed,
tears sliding
silent as cat paws tripping down my face.
I did not know why at first.

Confused I stared into the dark
forcing shapes to form in the air
until bulky and black they fell
into my open mouth.

I am starting to let you go?

And there is a version of me stuck in that parking lot
I rode a mechanical bull and hurt my back
the snow is falling, but I am not cold
so many beers in, and I am yelling into the phone
snowflakes freezing over, ice chips
biting into my cheeks, my lips...

I have kept her
a long time now, always
standing outside the bar, always
saying the same wrong things
the neon sign
awash in watercolor tears.

She will never be able to make you stay.

I watch you disappear into the crowd
around the bend of the hallway
I am staring at your name on my phone screen
in the dream the dial pad slips and stutters

I know your number though.

You did love me.

Paint over the picture, paint her over.
Pick a color—purple white green.
I feel mean, I told my therapist
just erasing the person like that.

But I never loved her.

I am trying though now, to remember
my own number, dial and say
I am sorry.

I tell her, go get a glass of water.
I say, get into the car and go home.
Please, stop listening to that song
with your head on your desk
and walk in the snow
while you still can make fresh footprints
before anyone else goes before.

Consequence

This morning I stood in between
the puff of breaths and pools
of ice that slipped away beneath me.
And thus, the hours go and
I have only to say to you
that I sought relief.

I have only to say to you
that I wanted to be hit.
That I deserved it.
That I beat myself,
merciless with my own blows.

I yearned for the time between snowflakes
the liquid gold-green of leaves in the late afternoon,
the lamps that lit the trees outside my window—
It was a woozy circling toward death.

And I wanted it all. Separate from you.

There was a time.
I used to ice skate.
What no one understood—
the fall, the purple spreading
ghoulish bruises—
that rough
kissing of the ice—

It was not a consequence
but was the goal,
all I ever asked for.

Orphic

of or concerning Orpheus

I have so many pictures of you,
but I can't quite remember your face.
Dare I look back?

Your eyes
I can see
with the car running
in my driveway, your head on my lap
I told you my favorite myth.
I stroked your forehead.

I want to take a shot and then another
rapid fire.

I had driven your car back
for the first time
you had a headache.

I want to be wasted.

When you knew me I was bad at liquor.
We would spit and make faces at each other.
By the end I'd have whole pints like it was ambrosia.

I want to turn you into a faceless mob
A mass of red eyes with gnashing teeth.

I wrote a story where I was never a drunk
and this scar at the base of my throat
is all smooth skin like when your fingers lingered
along my neck.

I was never a phoenix
but I know what it is to be reduced to ash.

That myth I told,
you didn't like the ending.
Orpheus never got Eurydice back.

At night I can hear him singing
and in my dreams I beg for forgiveness
and wake up warm until I know it was not real.

How could you still know my name?

Do you ever whisper it out loud
in the shower like a favorite song
you can't quite remember?

Orpheus sang all the way down then out
of the underworld.
All along was I singing for you?
He didn't make it far though
once he hit the surface.

I am sorry
for where I took you
even more that
I could not lead you back to open air
and sunshine.

Eurydice

I took a train pulled by cogs
up the side of a mountain
and sat in an outdoor cathedral
watching light filter through
green stained-glass leaves.

I was sober and 15
and I thought maybe there is a god.
I looked for him in the clouds
and the shadows dappling the stone.

More recently I have seen god
in full liquor bottles, unopened
and waiting to be poured.
And at their bottoms I found hell
a cliché, maybe, but the flames
still hurt.

I'll try to walk us out of it
I think we can make it
if I keep singing
and don't look backwards
for you.

Carthage

I see you pausing, sad
at the snow and our future
you see through windows
frosted over gray.
But I believe Hannibal
took his elephants over the Alps.
And I loved the stories of sowing salt
in your fields. Of burning and turning
on a spit until everyone's hunger
is sated.

We could stand on an ice floe
and fish together.
I'm no good at it, true,
but we'll use each other for warmth
to weather the blizzard.

But I believe in me
and you, and that
even lost amid
sharp peaks,
elephant's play in pools of water,
spraying up to the sky
and catching the drops on their tongues.

I will stand in snowfall in summer
to prove to you we will be all right.

The future is melting,
let's pour it into a glass
and drink deep.

Cleaning Tack

I've spent all day in the past
I polished leather
and rubbed a shining golden neck.
I found an old horse trainer's website,
he's judging now and
his rates are
exorbitant.

And I found your father's obituary.
You are surviving, it notes,
with your wife and two kids in Georgia.

And what has it all taken from me?
There used to be the burn of alcohol
and then just ash
to be swept up.
Now my partner
pulls my location up on his map,
reads that I have left the house.

To where? What end?
I am sinking mad like Ophelia
like a rock in a green-leaf stream.

I should give him credit
for putting up with me
the ugly wall color
the electrical miswiring
an order slightly off so that
the whole meal is ruined.

Pull the map up and I am sitting
blinking in a Dunkin Donuts listening
to you tell me it's impossible
for aliens to eat you
if you're wearing blue.

My doughnut was blueberry
I had a carton of milk too,
that was blue on the outside.
We weren't in love yet.

Last night when I saw it was only
half past midnight I cried out
how would I survive the night?
And dammit, I did.
Again.

I am pulling time like taffy.
I am barking like a mad dog
and everyone shakes their ears
I am a gnat.

Our kisses used to taste like barbecue sauce.
There is nothing more in the whole world
to intoxicate me.
It's a desert planet now.

My old leather bridle was so stiff
the noseband snapped.

It's OK.

I won't use it again.

Dunsinane

There are more gravestones
just past the BP
I hope they don't mind
their neon green view.

I picture them up close
in the dusk before night swallows
their shadows from the tidy grass.

At midnight they're far away
and out of sight in the dark
but in the morning,
they have crept up to my door.

Arithmetic

The sunrise shines pink
off of marble markers,
making rosy pools
in the green cemetery lawn.

The man gets up
to unlock the door
while they're measuring
the beats of our hearts
with tiny plastic cups.

I am tired of being condensed
and summed. I always hated numbers
and now, I am one.

Fractions of my life
add up but never make a whole.

I love the man
for opening the door
I love the people
lying beneath the shining graves
and I love the stars, long dead,
but still in our sky.

You can't drink love like water,
but I pour it down my throat anyway
and start to rise.

Red Rose Inn

The echoes of my life story
are bouncing around this old motel room.
They sound like everyone else's.
Hoarse voices joined in chorus.

One girl insists this place is haunted.
She hears noises at night
sees figures reflected
on her phone screen, feels clammy
hands grasping at her fingers.

But who of us
does not have a head filled with ghosts?
We bring them with us
and hope to shed them out
our eyes and ears.

I'm trying to make friends with mine
I feed them Jolly Ranchers
placate them with tiny pills.

They may wither in the daylight
but still they come at night
to curl up and whisper
never forget me.

Two by Two

All the clocks
announce different times.
We argue over which hour is real.

Quietly, inside a circle
of stiff metal chairs
we mumble prayer together.

Outside it starts to rain.
Will it go on for 40 days
and 40 nights?

Arkless, I have been swimming.
My strokes are faltering
my legs are cramping.
Maybe, have I found dry land?

But still, if so,
where is my dove?
Where is my olive branch?
Where is my promise?

Goats

The sun rose again today
and scattered pink among the clouds.
I could not take a picture.
I'll have to remember each
ripple of color.

The universe is not safe
and we are all vibrating
at different frequencies.
Will mine make you collapse
like hoofbeats over
an old stone bridge?

When it crumbles, it's true
it takes the hero with it
and, if they make it out at all,
the trolls beneath
need a new place to live.

And yet, as they emerge, blinking
they find themselves
happy—
they are out in the sun at last.

Underworld

The girl's body is covered
in dead people's names.
Hayley died in 2008,
Marcus made it to 2015
and Grace is adorned with flowers.

I'm counting my own names
they're written all over me
you just can't see.

Later, in the water,
I concentrate on being so weightless
I'll vanish into thin air.

Who will trace my name
over delicate flesh?
And who will think of me
when they see a horse
alone in a field
head bent down,
maybe to graze,
or maybe to pray?

Betsy

To my ex-boyfriend's daughter
who shares my middle name—
a taunt from a ghost—
I could have been half of you.

As it is there is nothing
in this reality to link us
and my life's fabric
is far too shredded to support
another—
a separate outside—
entity.

Sometimes...
it is so tempting
to go back,
swim through years as though
they were waves
and just shift things a little,
rewire one pulsing night
and end up with someone
else.
Not quite you, but a little
maybe.
Thin air and long sun shadows,
maybe,
but someone just the same.

You'd be too clever
too sad,
an imbalance
in the universe

but your eyes—
instead of green
they would be brown
just like mine.

You Were Right

I took a picture
of a memory we shared.
Thought of sending it to you.
Rejected the thought.

I kept your sweatshirt
it's too small now and doesn't
smell like you anymore.

I checked.
When no one was looking.

But still I couldn't
put it in that donation bag.

I came home on Friday drunk.
I smelled like it still and he knew,
full of disgust.
Memory wiped I passed out,
one more evening
obliterated, blown sky-high.

I have fistfuls of regrets.

Boxes of pictures with our faces
pressed together, decks
of cards you assembled for me
and still more regret scribbled down—
notebooks full.

But I wanted to let you know
after all this time
you were right.

I am always ticking, counting down,
ready to explode.

You were right.
To duck and cover.
To make your escape.
To leave me.

Fighting on a Wednesday

You're sitting at your screen
ready for battle
I felt so sick an hour ago
it was better when I could just throw
up the poison, get it out and then get on
with my day. But this is something
more complicated. It has to be nursed,
treated with dry toast and hot tea
And you're angry
You're exasperated
Your game is never going well.
We don't win, do we?
Unwilling
I used to write about white moth wings
and when I dreamt I had control
over the lava fields I was chased through.
But now I sleep hard and wake up screaming at I don't know what.
And I'm mad.

Remember in New Orleans on a corner when I still could just order
    a bloody mary at breakfast we caught a trolley to a graveyard.
We walked to the river and drank off the dregs of a fight with a
    few beers.
Now we have nothing to wash it away with, we sit
on the banks and just stare into empty water.

You like to say I always am. Anxious, scared, upset now angry. I
    always am. Medusa stared me down and caught
me in stone and frozen here I am screaming.

Flotsam and Jetsam

There are pieces of us
still scattered off the river exit.
I saw a dolphin
right off the beach
dipping happily
out to sea.

It's OK
to think of you still
sometimes.

I have always wanted
to hold onto that horizon,
to take it in both hands and tug
it out of the sky.

After you quit drinking
you're supposed to correct yourself out loud
every time you tell a lie

So,
I just did
the dolphin wasn't happy
and it's not OK
to still miss you.

I can start things sure, but letting them go
is not something that comes easily.

I lied again.
It is not something that comes to me
at all.

Watch your sugar
the doctor told me
so I ate an ice cream sundae.

I licked the whipped cream
off my fingertips.
I hoped it went straight
into my bloodstream.

I am starting things again.
But I've got to do my damage somehow.

I didn't lie just then.

The dolphin disappeared into the waves
I sent thoughts of welcome loneliness
and maybe I got some back.
What are you doing now?
I imagine collecting our pieces
and shoving them in that dumpster
you'd sneak to behind the gas station
on moonlit nights
meant to be romantic.

I dig myself deeper
wet sand stuck beneath my fingernails,
hurting a little,
until finally I hit water
and can swim to shore.

Funeral Procession

Maybe my brother-in-law will go out
and find love tonight
we used to go to parties now
we get no invites. The old man
in the Nirvana shirt is at the gym
again. I explained today how I don't drink
as though it were just something
I had decided on my own.

At least we could order
some Chinese takeout
pretend laugh into
moo shu pork. Leftovers
are always so dreary, I am
boxed up in stale
Tupperware kept at a cool 36 degrees.

It used to be so easy
just buy me a beer. I'm floating
in the sea. The ocean is filled
with ice. The waves are growing
long legs, hooves forming
necks cresting. If only I'd ride
them all to the line of the horizon
or at least across the river
to the bank safe on the other side.

I used to chant ICE and SNOW
and close my eyes to go
someplace else, where
liquids freeze and stop flowing
solid, reliable
until they melt
at least in tears
and flood the room and wash
me out to sea.

Used to,
who am I kidding—
still do.

Jokes on
who?

I always wanted to ride on a donkey.
Have one drag my coffin behind him.

Giving

When I was drinking
my days were wet
watercolors
smeared with hard-pressed
five fingertips
sometimes the colors melted together
and shone.
Other times it was just muddy
thumbprints littering the canvas.

I would wake up so early and start
then, while the sky was just lightening.
Fall back asleep wake up at noon
groggy half-sober
the world collapsing in on itself
I'd have to start again.

Now I'm not supposed to ever start
and the color has drained
from my days. Crystal clear they snap
in my face like half-mad animals.

There is a baby being born in Boston.
I called in sick to work because
I was really sick and still you made me
feel like I was lying.

Contractions are ten minutes apart.
It's not something I will ever know about.

These are our barren days.

If I betray you
it's just that I was trying
to paint in some color again.

Sobriety

The room is locked now.
The window is small.
One afternoon while you were gone
I drank and wrapped presents slowly
with each sip
the window widened—
the sunlight streaming in brought peace.

In California I was stone sober when we took
the old trucking road late at night,
the headlights catching branches
horror movie style bright white hands
thrown up against the dark.

You were slowing down for me
but still I felt as though we were whipping
around each corner without control,
dodging the trunks or trucks or looming
arguments we had yet to have.

We made it safely to the Pacific Ocean.
Alien waters far from home.
In the distance once we saw whales.

Happiness is never so simple as a stroke of hair,
a whisper late at night that I love you.

There's always also a lumpy mattress,
an hour lost on unfamiliar streets,
and of course the first beautiful sting
of raw alcohol against the teeth.

Repeat It Please

The voices,
in unison through the decades
gentle, but maddeningly stern
you need to learn to be alone.
you shouldn't really miss me.
It's nothing.

My stomach hurts.
I said before 3rd grade, terror
blotting out all sight
of the low red-bricked building.
My mother, bending
to adjust a seatbelt for a screaming
brother. Telling me
Just go ahead. It's nothing.
It's normal.

And I *can* be alone, curled
into my crystal cavern at 4:30 am
when I still have hours before
the sun invades
and the booze has smoothed
the darkness into a cool
quilt, wrapped around me
and just me
my shaking hands shoved
beneath the covers, my eyes
maybe glazed but now calm
can take in the moon
reluctant to cede its sky
just like me.

If I can stay here forever
where the minutes are only
mine where the stomach pain
is thinning and washing
away where I swallow

iced lemonade as though
I was waiting on a porch
for a long-unseen friend.
If.

But I go missing and you scream.

Isn't this what you all wanted.
It's nothing
It's nothing.
It's nothing.

And I'm safe inside it.

Lithium

The spring I choose to haunt
from the future is filled with it.
Young maidens come to drink
and leave humming.

But it is the donkey I show myself to—
whisper my secrets into his long brown ears.
He found his way here by accident
and he'll tell no one else
except that one girl
who likes to scratch letters into mud.

One day, while she's scraping out his hooves,
he'll turn his head and with a nuzzle
she will hear him

and I will hear him, only 12 myself now,
not a ghost yet, brushing out
loose dirt from sole, only to stop
and rest my hand on his soft nose.

I haunt myself.
All three of us just listening.

Narnia

You can't speak to me
the way the leaves can
in the wind.

I would mix it with peach juice
as though that might undo
any sinister effects.

I wish to get whisked away
by forces beyond control
off a train station platform
kicking my feet suddenly
by the ocean instead of
off a hard bench, on
sterile tile floor.

Instead, here
the sea glitters green
and in the distance there are
the final notes
of trumpet song.

Fountain

I was waiting for you,
our waters became green
and I could still feel my feet
and our waters are not blue.

You are a busy beaver
a good soldier.
And I took her hand, daughter of Eve,
led her to my home, gray cube.
My feet became hewn
hoof-like under lamplight.
I have been here for ten years.
The puzzle to be solved
is on the staircase,
but every day I wait for the elevator.
It only stops at three floors.
It is coming down now.

Please Hang up and Call 911

I go for a birthday swim
is it the chlorine or
have I been crying?
A fun guessing game.
Tag! Whenever I was it
I couldn't catch anyone.

Have I been crying?

I'll fall asleep to sounds of cooking
in kitchens far away.
There we are in a picture frame
full glasses of wine held tight in our hands.

If only I cup mine that same way
maybe one will appear filled
to the brim.

You scream.

I am a void, I'll eat you up.

I live with snickers coming down the hall,
strangled puffs of breath
invading each hour.
A lamp you tap to send light
across a continent. Rainbow
colors, teal and red.

It's true I don't like to throw things away.

I am a year older.
Still a trooper.
Still a soldier.
Have you ever been or plan on becoming

Please notify a doctor.

Side effects could occur
and we wouldn't
want
that.

Kill The Witch

When the ambulance came it threw swirling red
all over our house
like torchlight clutched by an angry mob.

You say you wore a path in the floor of that waiting room.
I was on my own, not sure if I wanted to stay.

The nurses kept calling you my husband
asking where were my kids and how many?

Wizard of Oz tornados circled around me full of precious objects.
People turned to chairs and back again,
small child ghosts crooned ominous warnings.

Single, I still check that box.

And I get up early. I watch girls try on wedding dresses. My dog
barks.

There is no one around now. My own sea to swim in. And I've too
strong a stroke to drown.

Don't throw me a line,
I've never been known for a light touch, and my hands are covered
in rope burns.

Let the house crash down. Kill the witch. The witch is me.

Lady Ghoul

I'll be the woman in white
on the edge of the trees
it's windy and you'll
have to squint to see
am I there or is it a wisp
of cloud blown off
into bare branches.

Don't remember me.
I'm burying my toes
in rich soil hoping the clippings
will grow.

I'd rather be known
as a birch tree, white bark
peeling while children come
to play and draw
crude monsters
on the back of my skin.

Portent

I am a woman
who sometimes has premonitions
and I have been itching for weeks.

We see things in the sky
did I see better slurring, unfocused?

Monsters moved for me in the dark
when I was small and alone and then
again two years ago in a hospital room
the beeping keeping time
with their pulsing red eyes.

They tell you not to forget it
but also not to think of it.
We stayed on a lake once in Washington State
that we couldn't swim or fish in
because our blood wasn't right for the land.
I can't blame it. I wouldn't want our blood either.

We are false, walking these trails unsteady
with high arched feet. I want to go home
where it is raining
and a calf is struggling to stand and nearby
on a jumbled stone fence
a raven lands
he thinks he is
unremarkable just looking
for breakfast but he doesn't know

he's an omen.

Fortune

I'm not a psychic but
I can read your mind from thousands of miles away.
That you wish, just a little
I had died. Made things simpler.
The memory of me relatively easy
in the past tense.
If but I had looked down on the cartoon Earth
that hung below me in the beeping bed
and shrugged and moved along
to some other planet.
Then you could have written a poem
about your dead
ex-girlfriend—
fiancé, I used to say
just so people would get
how serious we were once.

If I was just gone
you could count my hours safely
and put them in a jar
twist the lid on tight.
Instead you hear my whisper
from thousands of miles away
that I'm still here
still churning
still remembering
all those hours that make you up.
Atoms spiraling and bouncing
and sending your face
into my nightmares.

Take my pieces
my eyeballs
my fingernails
the locks of my hair
you joked about clipping.

Let's burn them
and draw the next card. It could be lovers
you wished for death.

I wish you had told me
my crystal ball was dark and cloudy.
I would have taken a knife
and cut my own wrists for you.

I Came to Say Goodbye

I keep dreaming of you,
that I've found myself at your wedding
and I'm plotting a drink
in my hand. I knew at 19
your ghost would haunt me.
You shed me like a few extra pounds.
You've kept them off so far but
old age creeps up, and the weight with it.

They've x-rayed and ultrasounded
MRI'd CT scanned me. I've been shot full
of iodine so they could get a clear look
the warm bloody taste filling my mouth
making me want to spit but there's nothing
there to stain the floors with.

They found some things, but no trace
of pieces of you. Proof that doctors miss
all the important signs. The body is just the surface
of a lake you're still at the bottom of.

I don't want to close my eyes again
to see your face saying
I could have done things better.

Today I'll swim a mile, cut through
the water that only resists a little
I can see you buckling car seats
making pancakes moving boxes
down a hall.

But today, too, the today that happened then
we are still curled up on my bed
staring at the star stickers on my ceiling—
on every 17-year-old girl's ceiling—your heartbeat
making me weak and sleepy our memory
fading, even as your spirit floats above
a sad sad look in his eyes.

I still know that look well.

Masterpiece

Life is
watching men dare whine
about how the Mona Lisa
is not as big as she should be,
complain about the girl snapping
too many pictures
having to wait their turns
not even seeing
what might not be painted there
the multitudes
behind her smile
that crashed into me
and had me pull my red winter coat
a little tighter at 20.

At 24 I had plotted marriage
26 I figured kids
but our scenes don't write themselves
like we scrawl them out in red crayon.

Our scenes always go
a different way—with a song playing
that we don't particularly like
and the camera panning around
the all too familiar room—
it's a mess!
We pause, carefully, on a cast-off shoe,
linger a long time
on an empty bottle,
accusingly halt
at a crumpled dress...
then stop dead
on a hand
hanging lifeless.

The legions behind what you can't see
crash down like waves
they are not small
or insignificant.

Light of Day

You've dragged me into the daylight.
I have not fared so well.
Scorched, exhausted I wait.

I did better in the dark
lost and hidden in my web
of caverns beneath
a lonely mountain.

I had it all written out—
my own mythology,
my cautious triumphs
my silent waltzes
my midnight howling
my hubris taking me down
by the heels.

I was the hero of my story,
and it just so happened
it was a tragedy.

Some stories are.

I delighted to play
riddle games in the dark
with travelers
I could never quite make out.

My croaking voice, my lantern eyes,
my thick slurring tongue.
Yet no one stopped to think
I might need saving.
They never stayed with me long.

But the story rewrote itself.

Some stories do.

My own abyss spat me out,
and foul and grasping for beloved gloom
I flailed into the bright world.

And now I have not expired, hidden,
but instead, exposed,
I twist in the open air
crunching sunlight
between my teeth
crying for the shadow kingdom
I have lost.

On Trial

You put on Garbage
at another age I listened to it
on another road
holding another hand
but that's all been said before
and we just blink and move along
shuffle along
looking at the soundproofed side
of the highway and wishing
to be some other place
until you are and then it's wishing
to be a different place from that too.

And I can't drink. You'd know and it would ruin
the day. But my hours are in ruins anyhow
the pieces I've tried to glue together
I never get it right, there's always an errant
bark too loud, an edge that doesn't
quite align, a syllable out of place.

And I can't but I could
walk across a bright parking lot
lay down my credit card.
Pour some liquid into my heart
to keep it beating—

THUMP THUMP THUMP
or is that the door.
A strange man is waiting outside
pulling his cloak tight
ready with his knife.

Partners

We say partners
and that I am not a good one.
Science has never been my subject
I wrote a whole essay about why ice cubes
melt and make our glasses overflow.
I didn't know it is frozen water
that takes up more space.

But certain things stick in my head
the glass in my grandma's windows is really liquid,
we were watching the squirrels
through a waterfall.

The seafloor is always changing tucking
crabs in before they become someone's dinner.

And light has to travel to humanity
through space. Some of those stars
are already dead.

Why the sky is blue, I heard in a lecture
once but I don't remember. We were outside,
staring up, and it was hot and I kept blinking
thinking about eating a chocolate
chip cookie and how green
everything is in a real Spring.

I do know
the moon tugs at the ocean from
its seat in the sky and plants
eat light, their green leaves
voracious.

I am always trying to be better.

You shovel in peaches,
cold and juicy,
daring,
and I sit and watch.

Now the ice caps are melting
and the oceans are rising.
Maybe I was never as wrong
as we all thought.

Red Light

The morning obliged
with thick mist
the liquor store was closed
but you're watching charges
and checking my breath.

You planted the bonsai trees
I gave you five years ago. One grew—a fresh new green soul
next to our kitchen sink.

Now, I'm driving through intersections thinking
lights can't be green
all the time.
Sometimes your touch
turns to raw panic nights
when I was left waiting
for just one
word
from you.

A woman said that to me 17 years ago
about the lights
I've been trying to write her into a poem
ever since, but she would never go—
still in hiding, on the run
from the awful husband the dirty trailer
the end we all know is there but still
we make it chase us until we can't.

Why did you plant them now?
I needed a new start back then.

I want to get married in a black and white dress.
A big one. Most days to you
some days to the cold wind off the saltwater
that wrapped me in its arms when I was 17.

I study the board. I'm always trying to save the dog,
preserve all the souls. You're trying to sink the ship.

It would have been nice. Champagne. A slow dance.

The magic of one well-timed word
a fresh green soul, a light,
an end driven through like new snow.

Stepmother

Am I the villain in your children's
bedtime stories? I'm just baking cookies
six hours away. It used to feel like an ocean
and now it feels like down the street.

And I have my own memories and you have yours
we've boxed them and wrapped them, mine have bows.
You were never one to care about mere appearances
until I got fat.

You could be my villain still, but
my heart isn't in it. Though you do feature
in my nightmares, I'm the one chasing
my own tail, teeth gnashing, arms extended
like a Frankenstein monster
I stomp over the same old grounds

and maybe in another life
I'm hunting pheasant, my tail wagging
as I race through the underbrush
hoofbeats sneaking up behind me,
I just need to get my jaw around
the feathered neck and bite down.

Vampyr

A drop of blood sets me off
like I'm a campy vampire
thirsting in the night
perched, perhaps, in a bell
or clock tower, pointy feet gripping
the rafters.

I turn around
there is no one there
a trick of the mirror
casting only a reflection
of a memory
nothing real or substantial
to touch and hold to my tongue
like a blood drop.

When I cried for you
I swore I would never stop
and that was back when
I kept my promises.

How to explain to my pursuers
that it's all been over now a long time?
That what I held once
disappeared in a hot puff of smoke
leaving me flapping leathery wings
chirping on a frequency
no one can hear.

Visitation

You rise up fast
an angry spirit
out of the exit off the highway
or a line from our song's chorus.
I can stare off in the distance
past you
but your spectral fingers twist
in my gut
your future
clear and bright
between the stars
we used to stand beneath
at the end of my driveway
we couldn't bear to say goodbye
do you remember the light
switching on sensing
our movement, I stood
on your sneakers and leaned in
feeling your toes wiggle beneath mine.

It all went the way of things
and now you haunt me
no sad spirit but angry poltergeist
you toss prized possessions
inside my skull, rattle chains
against my eyelids.

It would be a lie
to say I did not love you somehow still
that I don't remember what the snow fall looked like
twisting in lamplight that night.

But pieces are just that
they don't always make a whole.
Rattle the chains. Throw my picture frames
break the glass and I'll stare
at our faces. What we were once
we aren't now.

I will drive past the exit,
listen to a different song.

Still in dreams
I know your fingers will come sometimes
to tighten around my heart.

The Dig

I am excavating the past
throwing things out,
shifting others into my present.

I grew crystals once, glued plastic
gems to cardboard sprayed with glitter—
I'm digging pieces of the 80s out
of my skin like splinters
and then there are the remnants
of you.

The framed pictures
the poems carefully printed
on jagged unlined shreds,
the card with a dog in a bowtie
in it you had scrawled
I love you tons then told me
to take Excedrin for my headaches.

I can see you picking it out, a grimace
face rigid, sharp
grocery store lights resentfully
glaring at you.

It's easiest to forget that
we were both miserable.

I have been to weddings where they sang
of infidelity, of torrid affairs and the bride
and groom sat grinning jackals. That was
not us.

Thank God.

Usurp

When the heat of the afternoon
feels like a drink
a strong one
on the tip of your tongue
and smacks with the memory
of ice clinking along the side
of the pool as though it were
a giant glass to dive in
and even a swim can't
rid you of the dust you've collected
so many hours now, you've
been pretending not to count them.

And it seems like the nail ripped
from your finger will never heal,
it won't grow back—
will always throb and
when you splash the bleach
into the mop bucket
burn and burn
like your liquor used to.

As though you haven't been counting
the numbers of fingers on hands
thrown up in despair. This afternoon
or last or the next.

Both of you hang your heads and burn
as the sun sinks slowly
and all the shadows, hot to touch,
come out to claim their thrones.

Nimue

We used to sink to the bottom of the pool.
Scream out our secrets in bubbles and
rolling eyes.
It was familiar. I was used to speaking
through sheets of water

floating between me and the world.
And I was always knocking into
the backs of wardrobes hoping for snow.
Just one lamp would be enough
to light my way.

But it was always hot and dark
a sticky jungle filled with fangs.
And I am not the princess waiting in a faraway tower,
I'm the stepsister sawing pieces off my own foot—
forcing open wounds into delicate glass.

And maybe I don't have a happy ending
and my trail of blood
is what gives me away.
But it also is what you'll remember
years later as you're drifting off to sleep.

You'll leave me out of the story you tell your children,
but my pages always float to the top.
Even after I've long drowned, flowers
woven in my braids singing
every sad song we both know the words to.

The secrets I tried to share
No one ever heard.

Tour

In the halls of the Vatican
my breath started to leave me.
I looked frantic up to see a lion,
one paw missing and
I laid my hand as near as I dared—
splayed on his pedestal.

Maybe he winked maybe
the air was just thick then
and moving strangely
around the room.

Today you got some test results
your body refuses
any help offered up.
Spits it out with rolling eyes
and manic shouts.
You inhale hope then
breathe out poison.

And it wasn't the people pressed
from wall to wall or the booming
man at the microphone
warning us not to even think
of aiming our cameras up
towards heaven. They weren't
what made me panic.

It must have been the ghosts
screaming
at the gilded maps of their lost homes
or the lion wailing
over his lost foot
or Michelangelo himself
suspended high above us
a perfectionist
like you
driven mad by one corner lost
in shadow that he can't get quite right.

I hate to tell you
Michelangelo, muttering to yourself,
even long dead,
hanging over crowd after crowd
while the man at the microphone
refuses us entry to heaven.

I hate to tell you
but I don't remember your ceiling at all.

Only the lion with sad eyes
who showed me kindness
when I was out of air.

Adderall Song

The Adderall is wearing off
not the first time for me to live with
the surface breaches and the bottom diving
the focus lost like I was a thread
you just let go of
let's watch it unravel.

I want to meet a ghost
not to ask what it's like after but what
do I look like now in the gray twilight?

I am not a mother
with or without the capital M.
Tonight I miss the shots I used to take
against the dark the hard burn
of certainty, a guarantee
against the nightmares.

In the hospital I had so many
babies mine or maybe not
and they died one after another
pulled out from beneath me
red from screaming their last breath
and they knotted my wrists
to the sides of the bed
I was trying to save them all.
I am exhausted thinking of it,
and from trying to explain.

One me is standing at the wet bar
it is two am and she just needs two more
maybe a third, so easy to swallow
a ritual, a prayer in a shot glass

and another me is flailing seeing
monsters floating around her head

and yet another is writing things
on her school folders in heavy ink
over and over
violence is the last refuge
of the incompetent.

It didn't help me then

waves always crash
someone is always waiting
to throw a punch.

let me write it into a love song

let the water rock us both to sleep.

It is vital to recall
there were no nightmares
but also
there were no dreams at all.

Christmas Time

it keeps coming around and once it's gone
it seems silly to think it happened.
The whole world stringing together lights
bringing trees inside
and setting candles in the window.

California is lit with flame
I am on the opposite coast
the one with smaller waves
and sunrises. I cup my hands over my mouth.

Once all I wanted was your eyes
we'd get drunk and roll around together
I slammed a beer on the table hard in Paris.
I would marry him now, I said.
I didn't spill.

I often mean what I say
before it slips out of mind. Last night
I dreamed there were gin bottles hidden under the bed
my grandma kept coming in,
asking for a shot
the more I drank the more the bottles filled
until they were overflowing
making the room smell
like an open wound just treated.
I woke gagging.

It's the promise of a present that's best.
The chance that you might get what you want
after the paper's been torn away then
it's over with unless you peel it off, careful
not to rip, and save it for next year.

I've always been saving for next year.
Let's shred this until it's gone for good.

Auld Lang Sine

I am invested in ritual.

Abraham paused to sharpen his knives
allowing for the crucial moment.

I hear voices from the sky sometimes
whispering about stars long dead and gone but when I look up
they're still there.

What did Isaac think
when it was all said and done?
Did he dream of the sound,
knife blade across stone,
for the rest of his life?
Did he empty too many wineskins?
Did he get angry and beat his wife?

I used to drink here's to.
Here's to mopping the floor
to paying the bills
to your new baby that might have been
ours.

Here's to
this cup of juice that's enough
to carry me through the night.

I used to watch the clock numbers trickle along wanting to feel the
        world move
when midnight struck.
The ground never gave way though,
never gave an inch.

To high winds and mermaids
I was born to sit in a rainy sea.

I was born at midnight,
It's true,
my cries like steel kissing rock.

And with his eyes straight up
Isaac watched a star fall dead
right from his sky.

I am invested in ritual.

And tonight as the hour rings out
we start our new beginning with
a kitchen dance and
a ghostly hint of
lemon meringue.

Maine

There is snow on the ground and I'm
wearing a dress full of glitter,
weaving sequins into moonlight movies.
The stars aren't shining in your eyes though.

Sometimes tears come at the most
trite moments
the camera cuts away to avoid a hackneyed scene.

My college professor would not approve of this poem
I still write with her words stuck to my fingers.

So might as well embrace the cliche
zoom in
on the melodramatic blood
a sacrifice for good luck.
I always wanted to paint it over my doorway
but it's the wrong season for that tonight
and God has already sent his angel of death down
to some other place.
He's not with us here in Maine
and you have no flair for the dramatic.

You live still in my head—
old home movies always on rewind
moving backwards.
Who are you now so many years later
and who were you so many years before?

We are caught in amber
cut and polished
hanging around a lady's neck
she's running from soldiers in the middle of Prague
across the Charles Bridge
I've been there
you haven't.

So how would you know what time her heartbeat is keeping?

Fairy Lights

Trying to find my way home
some lights were windows
warm and waiting
others were pale blue
spirits calling me forward.

In one case I could not move
and I was seeing things that I knew
were impossible.
In a way I was delighted
beneath the horror,
vindication!

I knew magic was real all along.

And the Japanese fairy tale twins
looked at me with huge eyes
whispering
about the future.
They could see it.

The ground is frozen swamp, feet
snapping ice the branches thinning
as I creep closer.

And I am still in bed, the twins are keeping
me company, their heads moving
to the beat of the beeping
when I realize there is a third—
triplets now, the last one is weak,
twisted. She looks at me, sees I cannot move
tells me to run anyway.

I can't and the room is spinning
needles flying and circling in a Wizard of Oz
tornado that lifts me up, hospital room
chirping machines breathing tubes
and all.

I crash into the winter bog
that hundreds of years ago
I crept through so carefully.

The lights are bright blue now
and they are singing wetly.
The world has sunk beneath the waves
and I am one with this moment
in history. Where I face the warm
yellow of a home slumbering
and turn instead the other way.

Mermaid and the Wishing Well

You are saving my life
like in a 90's pop song
only really
without you I would have drowned
in the backyard pool
gin spilling into green chlorine
leaves floating down
to catch in my blossoming hair
and rest on my cooling forehead.

I still want it. Driving by
a place I used to go or when you yell
or when the doctors look at me
with a stern gaze
and tell me I am lucky to be alive.

You are my luck.

It used to be
consumed swiftly
whole pint glasses full
watching Little Women,
the one
with Winona Ryder
and when you came home you found me
on the floor. I could not even speak.

I always wanted a wishing well
but what could I offer it?
Pour out my liquor bottles
hear them clink all the way down
close my eyes
and ask for...?

Offstage

I am an omen
a black cat darting across the path
a raven casting shadows
from a high up perch
the woman in white dragging skirts
striding through the thick forest.

And you're rolling your eyes
I'm looking around the room for proof.
I've propped myself up on the well's edge
arms raised billowing sleeves
sliding past the elbows
eyes squeezed shut as I fall backwards
in moonlight.

Only to learn with a splash,
it was all offstage
it's the third act
and in the spotlight a man
is waving a shin bone in the air
cackling at the sky and stomping
his feet on the ground that's his.

No one was watching.

The raven calls out
in his left eye you can see your own death
and in his right a purple flower blooms.
If you put it in the right potion,
it will grant you eternal life.

You are rolling your eyes again.
The man is gnawing on the bone
the cat licks his lips.
The raven is a dot in the distant sky
and those stage lights were too hot
anyway

I am more at home here
with this cold water soaking
calling
cradling me down.

At All

I need to call *The New York Times*
to cancel my subscription
some part of me is always
dying of consumption
coughing up blood on a sun-drenched porch.

I like being able to read
the articles, but it isn't about that at all.

Black and white was always my thinking
tapping hard on the brain like a typewriter
the things you learn in a cold room, the words
thrown at you to help like bricks through a window.

They'll insist it's a life preserver.

I have been cutting myself on pieces of glass a long time.
I break things and
blood is the best punctuation mark.
It wasn't about proving you wrong at all.

In college we'd put bottle caps in our pockets.
To keep track, we said,
and walked home through the snow.
I was on the phone with you, passing
beneath the flashing yellow lights
at that one crossroads I lived near then.

They would be in my life
longer than you.

But this is not about those lights at all.

You didn't like talking to me drunk.
One of our many fights. Easy to forget. We have
to block our pain to perpetuate the species.

Or maybe it isn't about survival at all.

The truth of the matter is.
The Times is just too expensive
and I sure don't have any reviews coming out
any time soon to sit up
in an all-night diner, drinking coffee
wondering what the morning will bring.

And truth is
you laid out a towel for me.
A prince. A knight.
You know what I'm talking about.
Or was it just so we wouldn't get caught?

Turned out
we didn't need the towel,
and so what if I cried?
Blood is the better punctuation mark.

I don't think
it was about me at all.

Your Father is Dead

You wrote me love poems at 17
I'm coming up on 40.
And he writes over the sky pitch black.
Extinguish all the stars!
Everything looks better with the lights off
or after a few drinks.

Why do I still know your number?
I dial it in my dreams
until the screen glow fades like
an unused second language.

Why do I still want to call and ask
am I ok? Like you would know.
Only you would know.

Somewhere deep down
you're crystal-clear lake water, head bowed over—
frozen mirror.
But you were only safe
when we were balanced on a thin strip of land.
Now with waters rising
it's long swallowed up, I'm sure.
I haven't been back there.

Give them long enough everyone grows fangs.
Filled with poison I am a walking antidote.
I am here to save you all.

And the midnight sky is full of sun
if you go far enough north.

Here Are Dragons

I guess I have a type:
boys who pretend to be above sex
in cars but will oblige when you beg.

We had a windy night I thought
all I needed was you and then
later I had a night I took shots of gin
out of a mouthwash cap.
I was replacing you.
Which made me happier?
I can't even tell now.

I dream still that we're stuck together
in a parking garage
and I've killed someone or maybe
you have? Our lines were blurred
and indistinct.

I put "painfully single" on my profile
until someone told me it was too
pathetic. You were not alone.

There was cold weather when we fell in love.

I dream of getting married, but the dress is wrong
and they're serving only juice.

Don't worry, it's not to you.

I have a type I guess:
Boys who threaten me with suicide when
I might be pregnant with their child.

Frantic nights filled with gin,
I managed to drink you away.
And now I've stopped and you're back.

I have lived my life a scared rabbit
afraid your teeth would find my neck at last.

Maybe we will all decompose on hillsides but
what does it matter when once we kissed
in sandy moonlight. We'd just eaten pizza.
You tasted like tomato sauce and cheese.

We had times. And we tasted one another.
I've been burning my tongue and throat with raw
liquor for a decade just to change my own flavor.

I wish I had let you go before it started to go
downhill, all crashing down on rotting
bones and flesh and we didn't want to look
at the corpse or the worms that wriggled there.
But there we were. We fed them all.

I have a type I guess:
Boys with the same green eyes.

I fell off a horse when we were over.
I hit my head and sat in the back of a truck
while the EMT checked for concussion.
I hadn't let you go.
So I took muscle relaxers and a few PBRs.
I found peace in rotten sleep
and the newfound ability
to shotgun a beer.

Will I always be doomed to go back and
lie on the floor
of a 7-11 bathroom throwing up
bright blue Gatorade and wishing for death?

I guess I have a type:
Boys who like to laugh when I start crying
or retching.

You've done this to yourself now go
and rot. The Atlanta gate agent said
aw Honey you don't want to leave.
And I didn't.

But you did.

Gin, you buy it, and then it becomes
a part of you. Consuming you while you
absorb it into the bloodstream
instant comfort
that never lets you down.

At least not for 13 years when then suddenly
you're not just wishing for death
but praying against it
in a hospital bed and doctors are saying
you're bad and it's your fault and
never again
when they didn't care
much before and won't really after either.

I guess I have a type:
Boys who betray me in
my own hallucinations.

Don't tell me I'm wrong
for wanting joy to come to me
slow in the emerging afternoon
weather.

I loved you like a sea monster.

I'll rise again from the depths.

Just see.

Red Sky at Night

*"Birds sing after a storm; why shouldn't people feel as free to
delight in whatever sunlight remains to them?"*

— *Rose Fitzgerald Kennedy*

I have been heavy and dark.
Forgive me.
Once I was told I needed to hang on
for dear life
with my fingernails
and that is what I have done
but maybe I could have stood up
and climbed out all along.

I will remember my next dive
into the ocean.
I will love you coherently.

The moon will be there
and clouds will sometimes cover it.

Branches will bend and bend
and then snap swing
us back towards whatever it is
we desire most.

I will contrive no more promises
but pledge with my full heart.

I will see the world zoomed out
then in, narrowing, down to our
particular patch of blue and green.

We will be waving there.

Trivia Night

Four-years-ago-me is in the bathroom of a bar
certain that her double gin and tonic
is waiting for her at the table.

She'll make quick work of it and order another
then creep back in here with the toilet
and swig some hidden in her purse.

That me will stop to stare at herself
on the way back to her drink.

She's always pausing at reflections.
It's best to face your fears.

But today I shake the water from my hands and barely
meet my own eyes
as I rush to exit.

What's waiting for me tonight?
No gin.
A mostly full moon.
A clear-headed joke.
An argument fully remembered.
A trivia question about when
the Department of the Interior was established.

I knew the answer.
You didn't believe me.
I drove us home.

I was never good at word problems
they always seemed to me incomplete.
Why should you want to measure which has more volume,
the moon or the lurking glass of ice and liquor?
Why not just listen to the sounds they make
one tinkling against your teeth
the other humming into the universe's throat?

Four-years-ago-me ended the night alone too
having drank until no more sounds could penetrate consciousness
and the moon wiped away like a spilled drink from vision
and myself caught in my own bathroom eyes, bloodshot, blame-
    filled
unwilling to break my gaze.

Tonight I go outside and look up before bed.
The moon is there.
Not quite full.
I catch my own eyes in its reflection
tonight there is a pause
I do not know
maybe
I will like what I might see.

I do not know.
There is no glass of calm patience
no liquid certainty for me anymore.
The only sure thing is that
the Department of Transportation
was formed after the Department of the Interior
despite what you might think
about FDR and World War II
and that we will always
have a moon to look up at
and I can drive us home
when you have a headache
and now-me will do what
four-years-ago-me could not
and crawl into bed with you
and we'll both remember
and we might like that.

It is Time for Dinner

I am made of words
and dog eyes
liquid kindness, frantic
and often
apologetic.

Small, tiny—
I prayed to the stars
and created planets
of my own design.

To have loved
and been loved
by you, by others, even
briefly, even when
they put my shoes outside the door
and told me to go.
Was it enough?

We have seen the dolphins playing
off my own shore
and to share it with you
I have turned on all my lights.

The house is bright
I am calling you home.

About Atmosphere Press

Atmosphere Press is an independent, full-service publisher for excellent books in all genres and for all audiences. Learn more about what we do at atmospherepress.com.

We encourage you to check out some of Atmosphere's latest releases, which are available at Amazon.com and via order from your local bookstore:

For the Moment, poetry by Charnjit Gill

I woke up to words today, poetry by Daniella Deustch

Never Enough, poetry by William Guest

Second Adolescence, poetry by Joel Rolnicki

Z is for Zapatazo, poetry by Ruben Rivera

Until the Kingdom Comes, poetry by Jeanne Lutz

Warcrimes, poetry by GOODW.Y.N

The Freedom of Lavenders, poetry by August Reynolds

Convalesce, poetry by Enne Zale

Poems for the Bee Charmer (And Other Familiar Ghosts), poetry by Jordan Lentz

Serial Love: When Happily Ever After... Isn't, poetry by Kathy Kay

Flowers That Die, poetry by Gideon Halpin

Through The Soul Into Life, poetry by Shoushan B

Embrace The Passion In A Lover's Dream, poetry by Paul Turay

Reflections in the Time of Trumpius Maximus, poetry by Mark Fishbein

Drifters, poetry by Stuart Silverman

As a Patient Thinks about the Desert, poetry by Rick Anthony Furtak

Winter Solstice, poetry by Diana Howard

Blindfolds, Bruises, and Break-Ups, poetry by Jen Schneider

Songs of Snow and Silence, poetry by Jen Emery

INHABITANT, poetry by Charles Crittenden

About the Author

Caitlin Jackson lives in Central Florida with her terrier, her partner and their impressive collection of board games. She graduated with a Bachelor's in creative writing from Oberlin College and also has a Masters in Fine Arts from University of Central Florida. Sometimes, Caitlin still believes deep down that magic is real.

Throwing the Bones is Caitlin Jackson's third full length poetry collection. She has two previous published books, *Myths for Small Matters,* and *River, Run!,* as well as poems and short stories published in various journals online and in print. For more information on past publications and exciting news about future endeavors, visit her website at Caitlinjacksonpoet.com.